STEPHEN BIESTY

EGYPT

In Spectacular Cross-Section

Text by Stewart Ross

Consultants: Delia Pemberton, Joann Fletcher, and Edward Bleiberg

SCHOLASTIC NONFICTION

An imprint of

Dedia's family's house

Wennufer,
Dedia's father

Mutnofret,
Dedia's mother

Dedia

Aunt Meritat

Ipuia,
Dedia's cousin

Illustrations copyright © 2005 by Stephen Biesty
Text copyright © 2005 by Stewart Ross

Oxford University Press
Great Clarendon Street, Oxford, England OX2 6DP

Library of Congress Cataloging-in-Publication Data
Biesty, Stephen.
Egypt in spectacular cross-section / Stephen Biesty ; text by Stewart Ross.
p. cm. Includes index.
ISBN 0-439-74537-3
1. Egypt—Civilization—To 332 B.C.—Juvenile literature. I. Ross, Stewart. II. Title.
DT61.B537 2005
932'.01—dc22 2004059185

10 9 8 7 6 5 4 3 2 1   05 06 07 08 09

0-439-74537-3

Printed in Italy
First printing, September 2005

Contents

Egypt

the great
Nile River

Dedia's journey, 1230 BCE

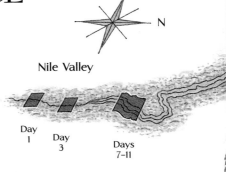

N

Nile Valley

Day 1

Day 3

Days 7–11

This is the mighty Nile River during the rule of ancient Egypt's powerful pharaoh Ramses II (1279–1213 BCE). Dedia, having just turned eleven, joins his father, Captain Wennufer, on a trip down the Great River. Delivering cargo as they go, Dedia and his father are sailing to Piramesse—the site of Ramses' magnificent royal palace. There, Dedia's uncle Nebre, a rich and important scribe, is getting married. Dedia is joined by his stern aunt Meritat and her know-it-all daughter Ipuia—not his favorite family members.

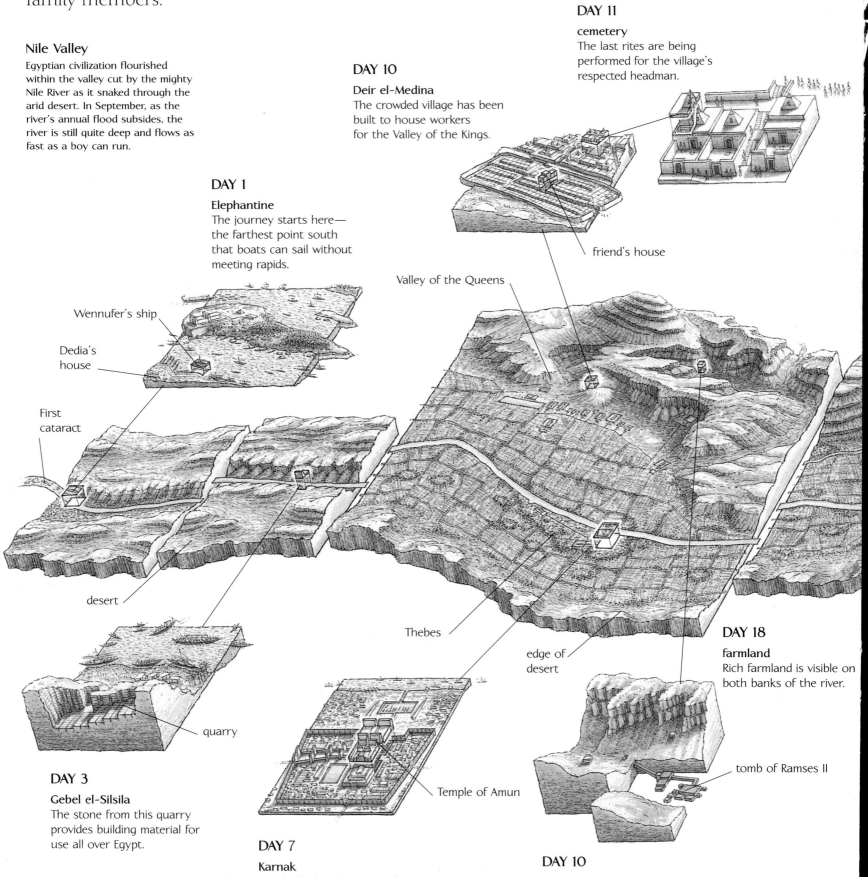

Nile Valley
Egyptian civilization flourished within the valley cut by the mighty Nile River as it snaked through the arid desert. In September, as the river's annual flood subsides, the river is still quite deep and flows as fast as a boy can run.

DAY 11
cemetery
The last rites are being performed for the village's respected headman.

DAY 10
Deir el-Medina
The crowded village has been built to house workers for the Valley of the Kings.

friend's house

DAY 1
Elephantine
The journey starts here—the farthest point south that boats can sail without meeting rapids.

Valley of the Queens

Wennufer's ship

Dedia's house

First cataract

desert

Thebes

edge of desert

DAY 18
farmland
Rich farmland is visible on both banks of the river.

tomb of Ramses II

quarry

DAY 3
Gebel el-Silsila
The stone from this quarry provides building material for use all over Egypt.

DAY 7
Karnak
Beside the broad waters of the Nile lies the most glorious temple in all of Egypt.

Temple of Amun

DAY 10
Valley of the Kings
In this secret site of royal burials, craftsmen are preparing a tomb for the king, His Majesty Ramses II.

Nile Delta

Day 18

Day 22

Day 24

Day 30

500 miles

800 km

The Egyptian calendar

The 360 normal days of the Egyptian year were divided into twelve equal months:

year   month   day

and into three seasons:

Inundation   winter   summer

Numbers were built up using symbols. An upside-down horseshoe-shaped sign represented 10. The calendar started over with each new reign. So 1278 BCE, the second year of the reign of Ramses II, was written like this:

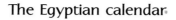

year 2   winter   under   Ramses II
                            of

month 2   day 22   the majesty   the king of Upper and Lower Egypt

Our story is set in the 48th year of the reign of Ramses II (1230 BCE).

DAY 24

Giza
The famous monuments of Giza are visible beyond the rich farmland of the riverbank.

Fayum

Lake Moeris

village

villages

Memphis

farmland

coast

marsh

lakes

DAY 22

Step Pyramid at Saqqara
The king's son is currently restoring the site of the ancient Step Pyramid.

Nile Delta
As it nears the flat and marshy coastline of the Mediterranean Sea, the river divides into several streams. These form the fanlike shape of the fourth letter of the Greek alphabet, a delta.

DAY 30

Piramesse
Ramses' royal palace at Piramesse stands on the broad delta of the Nile.

audience rooms

The harbor at Elephantine

Dedia has often visited the busy docks at Elephantine, but only to watch the ships in the harbor. This time it is for real. They are setting sail for Lower Egypt, where the Nile meets the Mediterranean Sea. Feeling anxious, Dedia clutches the amulet his mother has given him for the gods' protection. Aunt Meritat and Cousin Ipuia are running late. To keep their tight schedule, Dedia and his father leave without them. Dedia is only too happy!

amulet
An amulet was a small magic charm worn to protect its owner from harm or to give him or her special powers.

obelisk barge
A gigantic barge, towed by smaller rowing boats, is transporting a 1,000-ton granite obelisk that has been cut from the nearby quarry.

mast

lookout

cabin of woven reeds

caged baboon

Dedia wearing amulet

steering oars

storehouses

trading ships

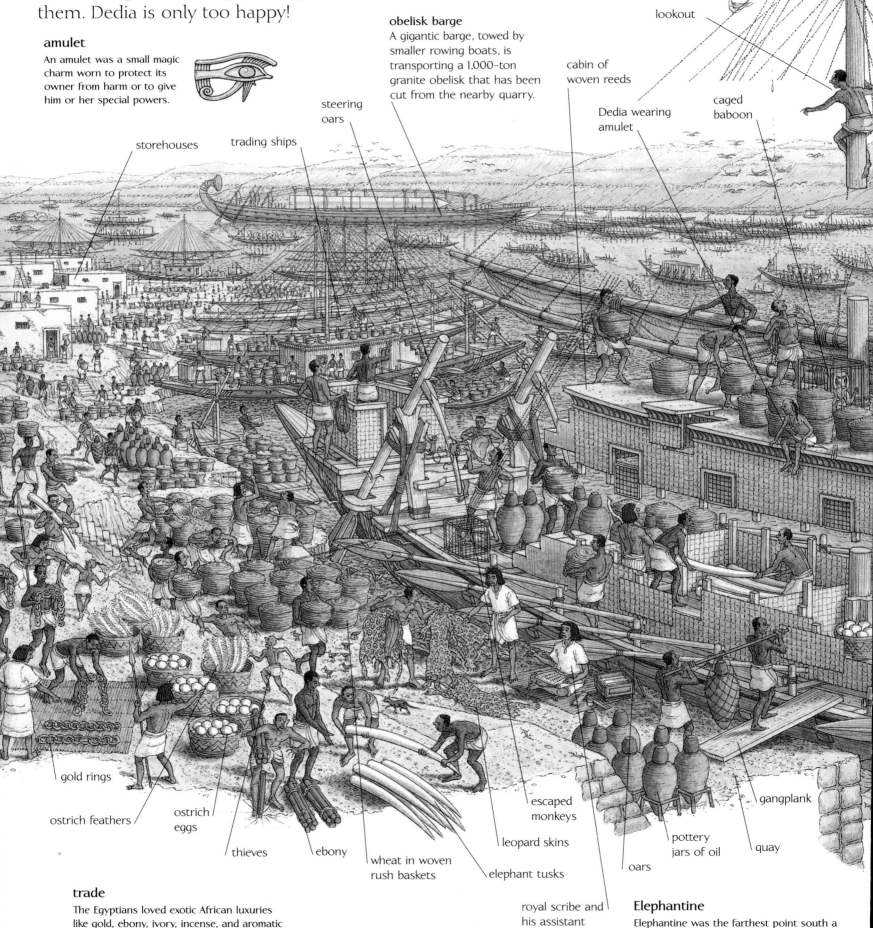

gold rings

ostrich feathers

ostrich eggs

thieves

ebony

wheat in woven rush baskets

elephant tusks

escaped monkeys

leopard skins

oars

pottery jars of oil

gangplank

quay

royal scribe and his assistant

trade
The Egyptians loved exotic African luxuries like gold, ebony, ivory, incense, and aromatic myrrh. As they did not use coins, they bartered goods instead of buying and selling them.

Elephantine
Elephantine was the farthest point south a ship could sail up the river without meeting rapids. This made it a major trading post for African goods.

cataracts

The first of the Nile's six cataracts—rocky rapids impassable to ships—was just south of Elephantine. At a cataract a ship was hauled from the river and dragged to the next stretch of smooth water.

rope made from plant fibers

wealthy lady in her private barge

Nilometer

Nilometers accurately measure the height of the river. This one consists of steps that the water covers or reveals as it rises and falls. Nilometers may have been used to estimate taxes—a high flood may have meant more arable land the next harvest, so increased taxes!

Day 1

temple of Khnum

The ram-headed potter god Khnum is Elephantine's main deity. Because rams are associated with fertility and potters with making things, Khnum is also seen as a creator god.

Khnum

rowers

palm trees

prisoners of war

ship's toilet

mud-sealed jars of incense

Wennufer

dom nuts—the fruit of the dom palm used in cooking

stone ballast to keep the ship upright

ship construction

Ships were made of long planks tied together over a skeleton of beams. Rectangular linen sails, mainly used for upstream travel, were hung between two wooden poles. Oars made the boat faster and helped with steering.

Quarrying at Gebel el-Silsila

Their first stop is at the Gebel el-Silsila stone quarries. While the ship's supplies are being unloaded, Dedia sneaks a closer look. The skill of the workmen—many of them slaves—is amazing. Imagine hacking out a block of stone exactly square—incredible! Aunt Meritat has taken another boat and has caught up with Dedia and Wennufer. Cousin Ipuia is there, too. She has brought along an unusual wedding present for Uncle Nebre—a live lion cub.

sailing upstream

baskets of grain—the workers' wages

Wennufer organizing the unloading of cargo

quay

slavery
Slaves were normally debtors or prisoners of war. They were not necessarily badly treated. Many worked as household servants, and fortunate ones even owned their own land.

singing
The oarsmen sing to help keep the rhythm of their rowing.

ferry

stone blocks being taken downstream

papyrus skiff

fishing
Some fish may not be caught because they are sacred—but the situation varies from region to region.

hippo

maid with ostrich-feather fan

lion cub

Dedia

Aunt Meritat

Ipuia

roast gazelle

ramp

linen awning

hippo hunt
Hippo hunting is a popular activity, although only males are supposed to be killed. The female hippo is associated with the household goddess Taweret, known as "the great female."

crocodile attack
Attack by Nile crocodiles is a real danger. Nevertheless, killing a crocodile is not approved of in areas that worship the crocodile god Sobek.

tools
In Dedia's time, tools were made of stone, wood, or bronze, a mixture of copper (about 90–95%) and tin (about 5–10%). A bronze chisel soon went blunt when it was hammered into stone.

sled and levers

mason's mallet

wooden wedge

stone pounder

bronze or copper chisels

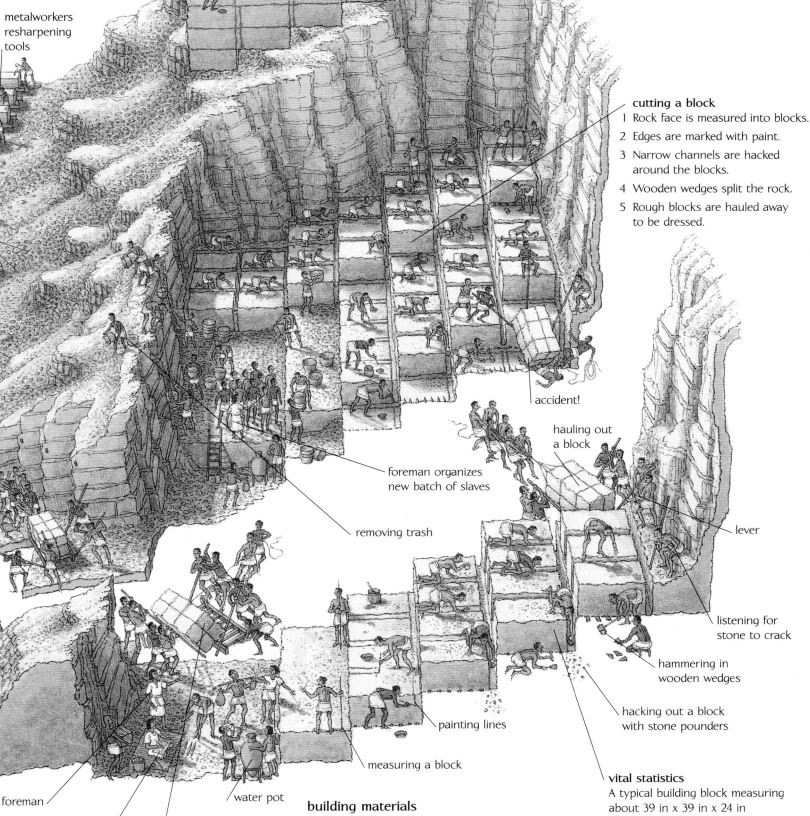

quarry workers
The backbreaking work of quarrying may be carried out by convicts or slaves. The more skillful tasks are done by trained workmen.

dressing
Mined blocks are dressed —cut to an exact shape. This involves hours of slow and painstaking work with a wooden mallet, bronze chisel, or stone ax.

metalworkers resharpening tools

mines and quarries
Egypt had many mines and quarries. Some provided stone suitable for large buildings like pyramids or temples. Others provided minerals, such as natron and salt. The most valuable yielded metals and semiprecious stones.

cutting a block
1 Rock face is measured into blocks.
2 Edges are marked with paint.
3 Narrow channels are hacked around the blocks.
4 Wooden wedges split the rock.
5 Rough blocks are hauled away to be dressed.

accident!

hauling out a block

foreman organizes new batch of slaves

removing trash

lever

listening for stone to crack

hammering in wooden wedges

hacking out a block with stone pounders

painting lines

measuring a block

foreman

scribe

water pot

maneuvering a block onto a sled using wooden levers

building materials
Egypt's primary building materials were mud-brick, wood, and stone. Gebel el-Silsila provided sandstone, which was easy to dig out. Limestone and basalt were other popular building stones. Granite, the toughest type of stone, was also the hardest to work.

vital statistics
A typical building block measuring about 39 in x 39 in x 24 in weighs about 2 tons.

Amun-Ra's temple at Karnak

The temple at Karnak, their next stop, is awe-inspiring. The group senses the mighty Amun-Ra, the King of the Gods, everywhere. Dedia and Ipuia go with Wennufer to deliver gold, ivory, and leopard skins to the temple stores.

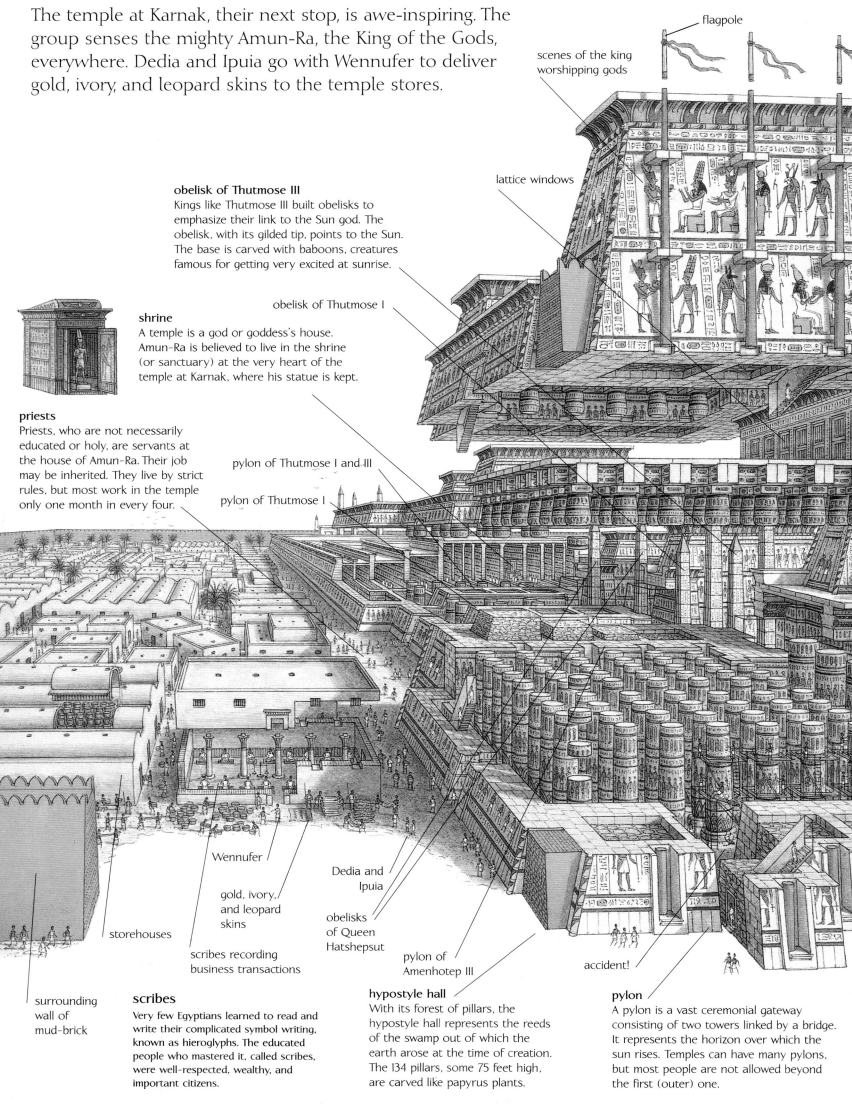

flagpole

scenes of the king worshipping gods

lattice windows

obelisk of Thutmose III
Kings like Thutmose III built obelisks to emphasize their link to the Sun god. The obelisk, with its gilded tip, points to the Sun. The base is carved with baboons, creatures famous for getting very excited at sunrise.

obelisk of Thutmose I

shrine
A temple is a god or goddess's house. Amun-Ra is believed to live in the shrine (or sanctuary) at the very heart of the temple at Karnak, where his statue is kept.

priests
Priests, who are not necessarily educated or holy, are servants at the house of Amun-Ra. Their job may be inherited. They live by strict rules, but most work in the temple only one month in every four.

pylon of Thutmose I and III

pylon of Thutmose I

Wennufer

Dedia and Ipuia

gold, ivory, and leopard skins

obelisks of Queen Hatshepsut

storehouses

scribes recording business transactions

pylon of Amenhotep III

accident!

surrounding wall of mud-brick

scribes
Very few Egyptians learned to read and write their complicated symbol writing, known as hieroglyphs. The educated people who mastered it, called scribes, were well-respected, wealthy, and important citizens.

hypostyle hall
With its forest of pillars, the hypostyle hall represents the reeds of the swamp out of which the earth arose at the time of creation. The 134 pillars, some 75 feet high, are carved like papyrus plants.

pylon
A pylon is a vast ceremonial gateway consisting of two towers linked by a bridge. It represents the horizon over which the sun rises. Temples can have many pylons, but most people are not allowed beyond the first (outer) one.

14

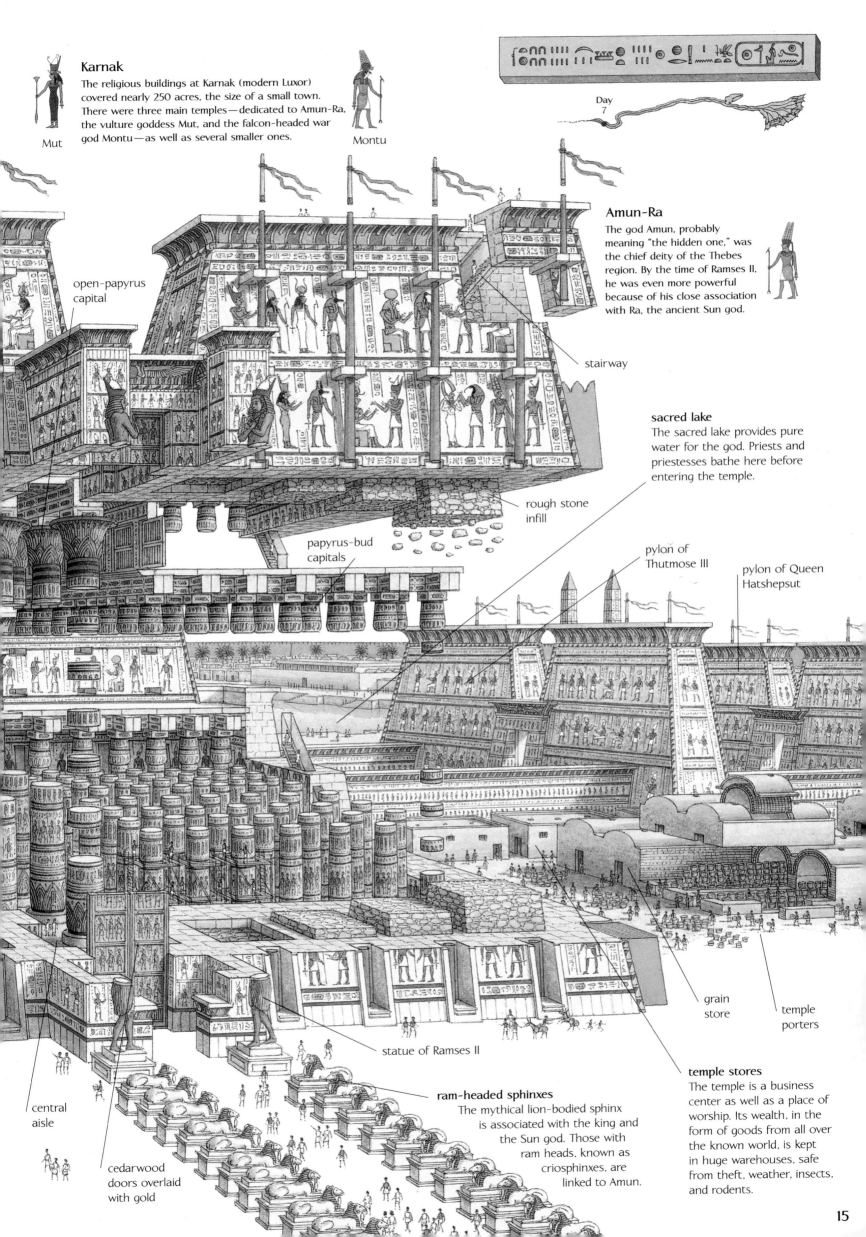

Karnak

The religious buildings at Karnak (modern Luxor) covered nearly 250 acres, the size of a small town. There were three main temples—dedicated to Amun-Ra, the vulture goddess Mut, and the falcon-headed war god Montu—as well as several smaller ones.

Mut

Montu

Day 7

Amun-Ra

The god Amun, probably meaning "the hidden one," was the chief deity of the Thebes region. By the time of Ramses II, he was even more powerful because of his close association with Ra, the ancient Sun god.

open-papyrus capital

stairway

sacred lake

The sacred lake provides pure water for the god. Priests and priestesses bathe here before entering the temple.

rough stone infill

papyrus-bud capitals

pylon of Thutmose III

pylon of Queen Hatshepsut

grain store

temple porters

statue of Ramses II

ram-headed sphinxes

The mythical lion-bodied sphinx is associated with the king and the Sun god. Those with ram heads, known as criosphinxes, are linked to Amun.

temple stores

The temple is a business center as well as a place of worship. Its wealth, in the form of goods from all over the known world, is kept in huge warehouses, safe from theft, weather, insects, and rodents.

central aisle

cedarwood doors overlaid with gold

15

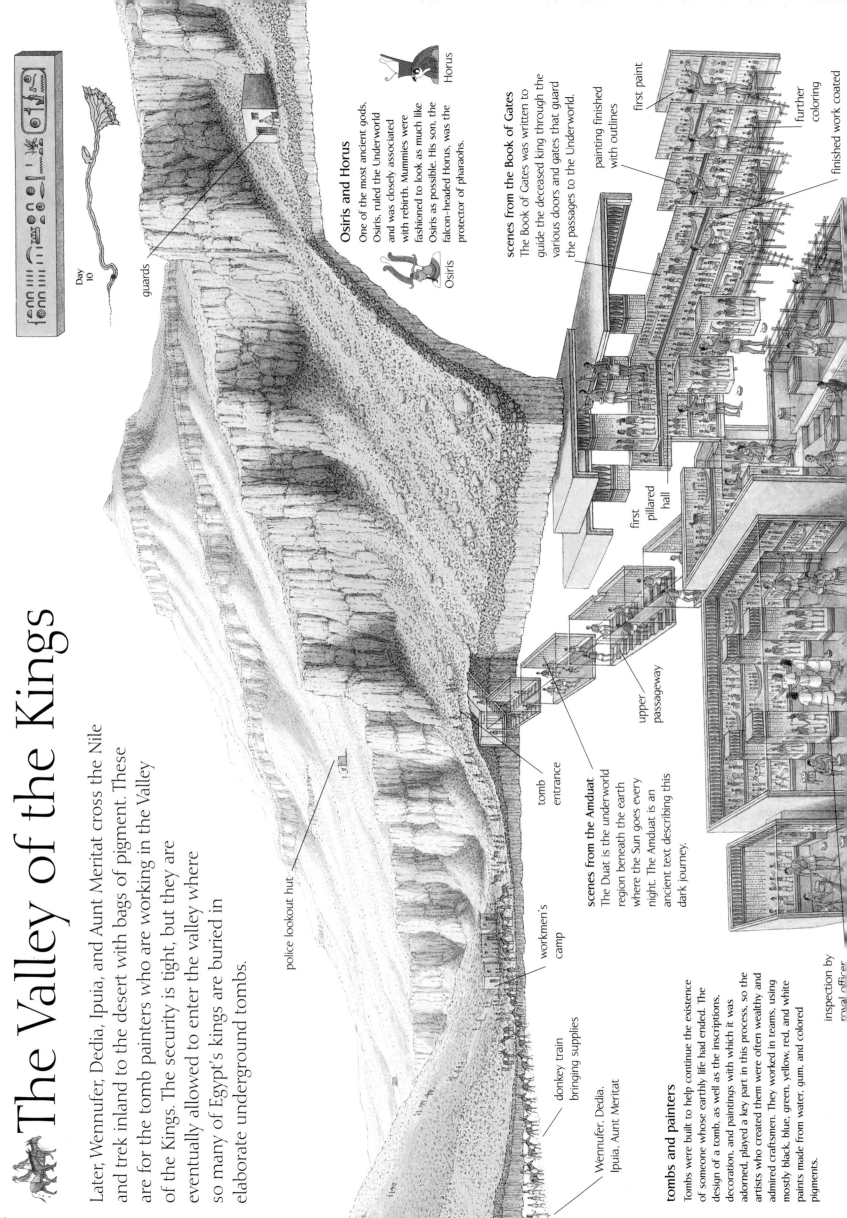

The Valley of the Kings

Later, Wennufer, Dedia, Ipuia, and Aunt Meritat cross the Nile and trek inland to the desert with bags of pigment. These are for the tomb painters who are working in the Valley of the Kings. The security is tight, but they are eventually allowed to enter the valley where so many of Egypt's kings are buried in elaborate underground tombs.

Day 10

guards

police lookout hut

workmen's camp

donkey train bringing supplies

Wennufer, Dedia, Ipuia, Aunt Meritat

Osiris and Horus

One of the most ancient gods, Osiris, ruled the Underworld and was closely associated with rebirth. Mummies were fashioned to look as much like Osiris as possible. His son, the falcon-headed Horus, was the protector of pharaohs.

Horus

Osiris

scenes from the Book of Gates

The Book of Gates was written to guide the deceased king through the various doors and gates that guard the passages to the Underworld.

painting finished with outlines

first paint

further coloring

finished work coated

first pillared hall

tomb entrance

upper passageway

scenes from the Amduat

The Duat is the underworld region beneath the earth where the Sun goes every night. The Amduat is an ancient text describing this dark journey.

tombs and painters

Tombs were built to help continue the existence of someone whose earthly life had ended. The design of a tomb, as well as the inscriptions, decoration, and paintings with which it was adorned, played a key part in this process, so the artists who created them were often wealthy and admired craftsmen. They worked in teams, using mostly black, blue, green, yellow, red, and white paints made from water, gum, and colored pigments.

inspection by royal officer

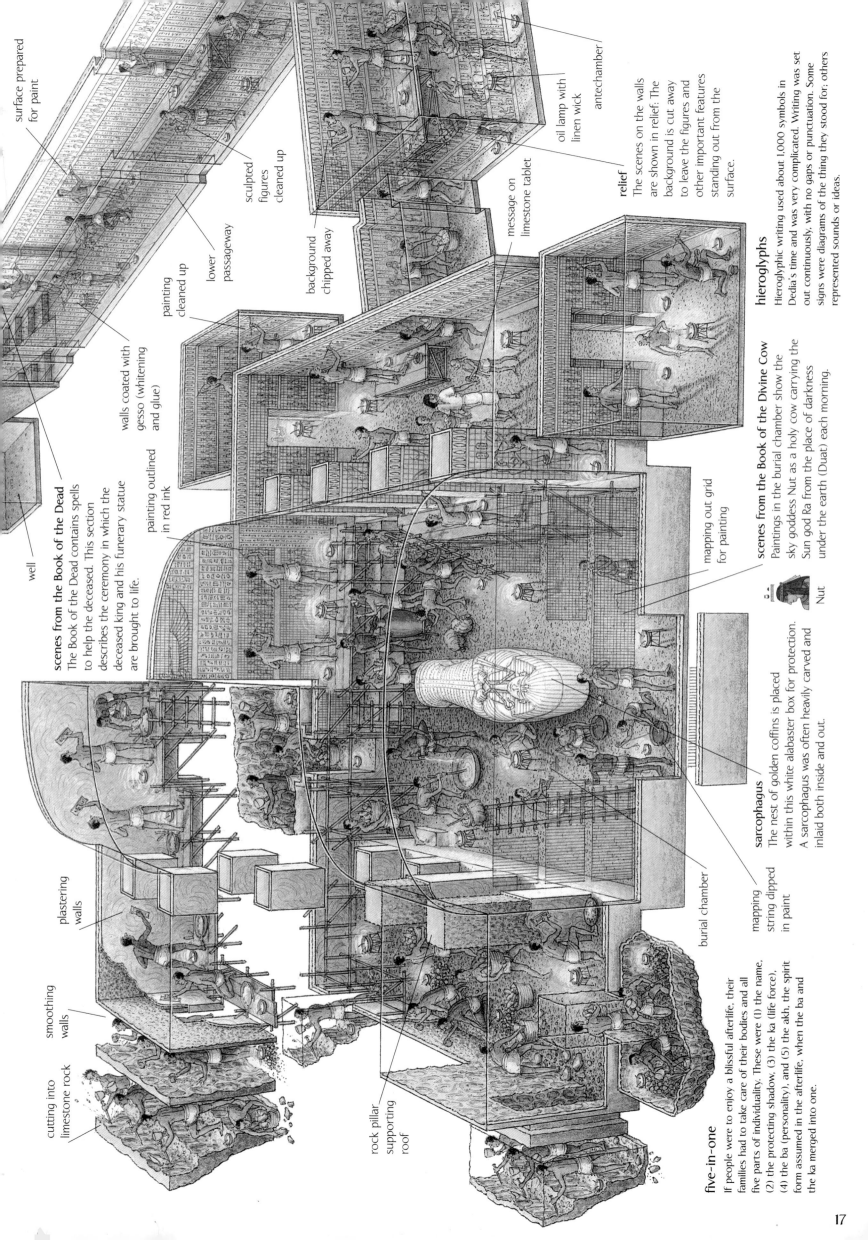

surface prepared for paint

well

sculpted figures cleaned up

lower passageway

painting cleaned up

walls coated with gesso (whitening and glue)

background chipped away

painting outlined in red ink

scenes from the Book of the Dead
The Book of the Dead contains spells to help the deceased. This section describes the ceremony in which the deceased king and his funerary statue are brought to life.

plastering walls

smoothing walls

cutting into limestone rock

five-in-one
If people were to enjoy a blissful afterlife, their families had to take care of their bodies and all five parts of individuality. These were (1) the name, (2) the protecting shadow, (3) the ka (life force), (4) the ba (personality), and (5) the akh, the spirit form assumed in the afterlife, when the ba and the ka merged into one.

rock pillar supporting roof

burial chamber

mapping string dipped in paint

sarcophagus
The nest of golden coffins is placed within this white alabaster box for protection. A sarcophagus was often heavily carved and inlaid both inside and out.

mapping out grid for painting

scenes from the Book of the Divine Cow
Paintings in the burial chamber show the sky goddess Nut as a holy cow carrying the Sun god Ra from the place of darkness under the earth (Duat) each morning.

Nut

oil lamp with linen wick

antechamber

message on limestone tablet

relief
The scenes on the walls are shown in relief: The background is cut away to leave the figures and other important features standing out from the surface.

hieroglyphs
Hieroglyphic writing used about 1,000 symbols in Dedia's time and was very complicated. Writing was set out continuously, with no gaps or punctuation. Some signs were diagrams of the thing they stood for; others represented sounds or ideas.

17

Deir el-Medina stopover

After visiting the Valley of the Kings, Aunt Meritat is tired and Ipuia misses her lion cub, so they return to the boat with their servants. Dedia and his father visit the nearby town of Deir el-Medina (which houses the workers in the Valley of the Kings). In Deir el-Medina, Dedia and his father go to see an old family friend. He makes them feel welcome and invites them to stay the night. Dedia is quite relieved to have one night away from Ipuia's endless chatter!

toys
Egyptian children played with simple toys such as balls, dolls, spinning tops, and model animals.

air vent on the roof to catch the breeze and direct cool air into the rooms below

walls of mud-brick

drying fish

rush mats

wood ash added to grain to keep off pests

spinning tops

accident!

linen chest

rolled-up sleeping mats

painting a funeral chest

clean clothes delivered by laundryman

water delivery

Dedia

Wennufer

host

hall

shrine for ancestor worship

furniture
The best furniture was made from wood, elegantly carved, and painted. Ordinary homes had to make do with mud-brick benches, a few stools, and clay pots and rush baskets for storage.

security
Windows had no glass. Their small size helped keep the house cool and secure. For added protection against thieves and animals, they might also be covered with stone grates. The entrance to the cellar, where valuables were kept, was often protected by placing a bed over it.

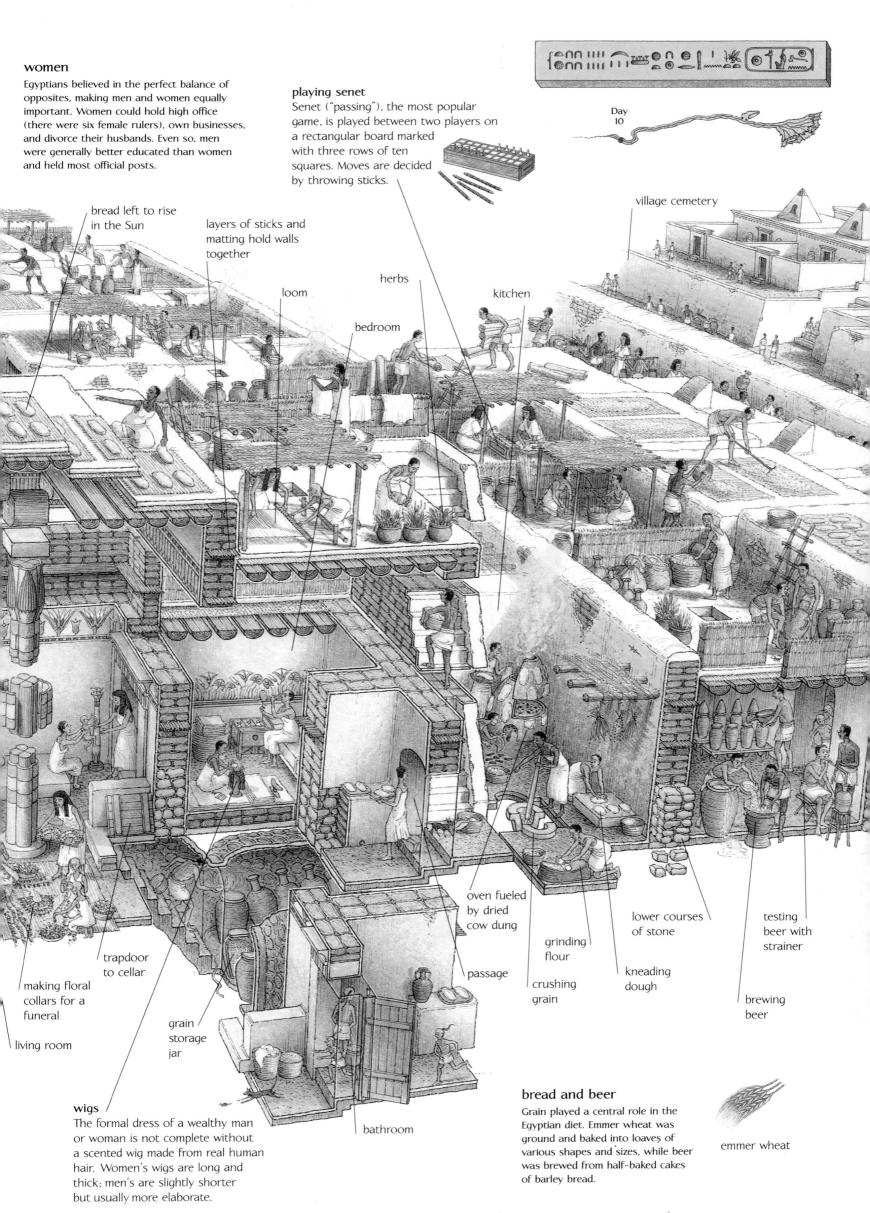

women

Egyptians believed in the perfect balance of opposites, making men and women equally important. Women could hold high office (there were six female rulers), own businesses, and divorce their husbands. Even so, men were generally better educated than women and held most official posts.

playing senet

Senet ("passing"), the most popular game, is played between two players on a rectangular board marked with three rows of ten squares. Moves are decided by throwing sticks.

Day
10

village cemetery

bread left to rise
in the Sun

layers of sticks and
matting hold walls
together

herbs

loom

kitchen

bedroom

making floral
collars for a
funeral

living room

trapdoor
to cellar

wigs

grain
storage
jar

bathroom

oven fueled
by dried
cow dung

passage

grinding
flour

crushing
grain

kneading
dough

lower courses
of stone

testing
beer with
strainer

brewing
beer

wigs

The formal dress of a wealthy man or woman is not complete without a scented wig made from real human hair. Women's wigs are long and thick; men's are slightly shorter but usually more elaborate.

bread and beer

Grain played a central role in the Egyptian diet. Emmer wheat was ground and baked into loaves of various shapes and sizes, while beer was brewed from half-baked cakes of barley bread.

emmer wheat

19

A funeral at Deir el-Medina

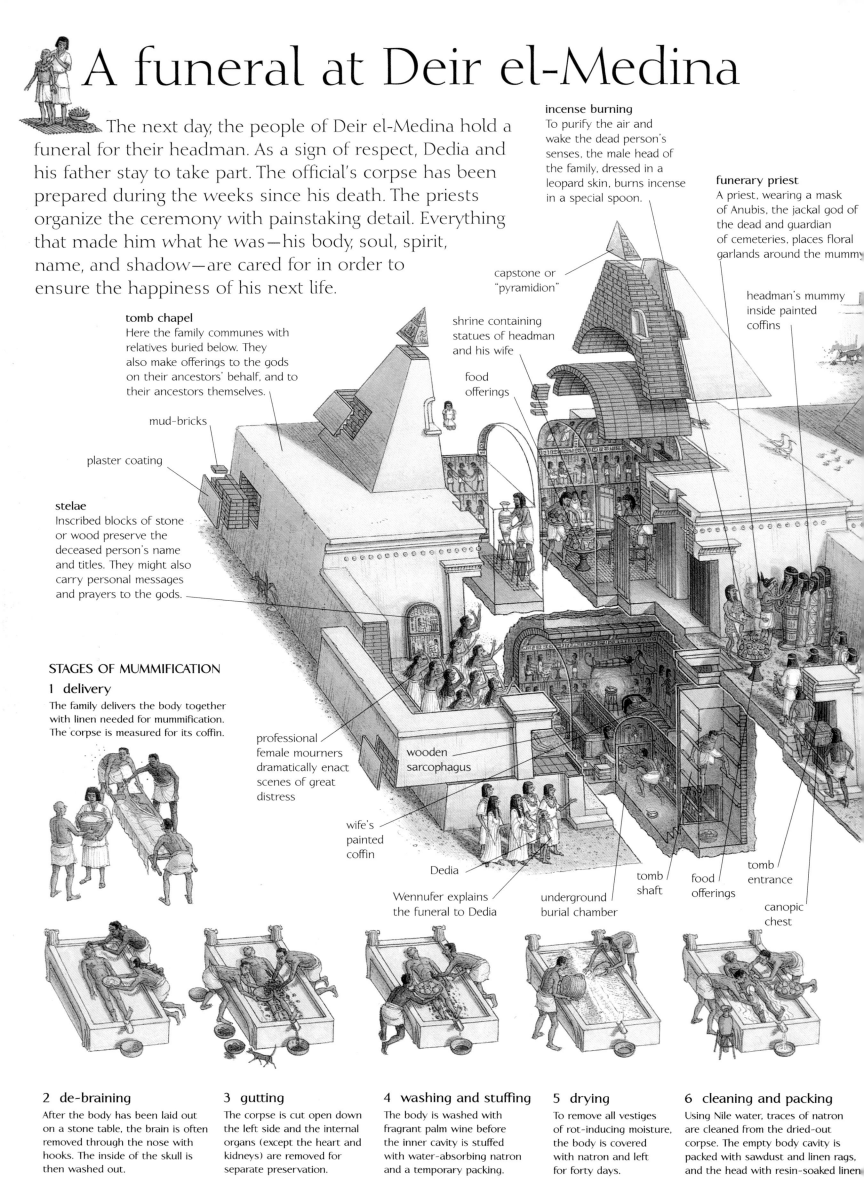

The next day, the people of Deir el-Medina hold a funeral for their headman. As a sign of respect, Dedia and his father stay to take part. The official's corpse has been prepared during the weeks since his death. The priests organize the ceremony with painstaking detail. Everything that made him what he was—his body, soul, spirit, name, and shadow—are cared for in order to ensure the happiness of his next life.

incense burning
To purify the air and wake the dead person's senses, the male head of the family, dressed in a leopard skin, burns incense in a special spoon.

funerary priest
A priest, wearing a mask of Anubis, the jackal god of the dead and guardian of cemeteries, places floral garlands around the mummy

capstone or "pyramidion"

shrine containing statues of headman and his wife

food offerings

headman's mummy inside painted coffins

tomb chapel
Here the family communes with relatives buried below. They also make offerings to the gods on their ancestors' behalf, and to their ancestors themselves.

mud-bricks

plaster coating

stelae
Inscribed blocks of stone or wood preserve the deceased person's name and titles. They might also carry personal messages and prayers to the gods.

STAGES OF MUMMIFICATION

1 delivery
The family delivers the body together with linen needed for mummification. The corpse is measured for its coffin.

professional female mourners dramatically enact scenes of great distress

wooden sarcophagus

wife's painted coffin

Dedia

Wennufer explains the funeral to Dedia

underground burial chamber

tomb shaft

food offerings

tomb entrance

canopic chest

2 de-braining
After the body has been laid out on a stone table, the brain is often removed through the nose with hooks. The inside of the skull is then washed out.

3 gutting
The corpse is cut open down the left side and the internal organs (except the heart and kidneys) are removed for separate preservation.

4 washing and stuffing
The body is washed with fragrant palm wine before the inner cavity is stuffed with water-absorbing natron and a temporary packing.

5 drying
To remove all vestiges of rot-inducing moisture, the body is covered with natron and left for forty days.

6 cleaning and packing
Using Nile water, traces of natron are cleaned from the dried-out corpse. The empty body cavity is packed with sawdust and linen rags, and the head with resin-soaked linen

journey to the afterlife

In a final judgment after death, a person's heart was balanced against the feather of Maat (truth) to see if they were worthy of entering the afterlife. The hearts of those who failed were flung to a hideous monster known as the "Devourer." Those who succeeded were allowed to proceed to the Field of Reeds, the kingdom of Osiris.

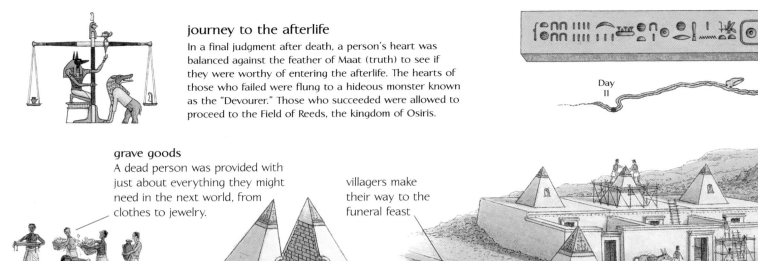

Day 11

grave goods

A dead person was provided with just about everything they might need in the next world, from clothes to jewelry.

villagers make their way to the funeral feast

clay seals
Often stamped with the image of Anubis, seals protect the locked doors to the tomb.

canopic chest
The corpse's internal organs (except the heart and kidneys, which are left in the body) have been mummified and stored in canopic jars. These are assembled in the canopic chest.

courtyard

white ox and sled return to the village after delivering the coffin

friends and relatives, wearing white headbands, prepare to escort the body

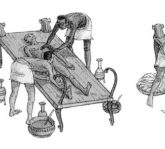

7 oiling
The body is transferred to a wooden table. Here its skin is rubbed with oils, the nose holes plugged, the eye sockets stuffed, and a final coating of resin applied.

8 wrapping
Reciting spells at each stage, the embalmers start to bandage the body, beginning with the limbs.

9 protecting
In a process that takes many days, the entire corpse is wrapped in hundreds of yards of linen bandages. Protective amulets are placed within the bandaging.

10 securing
The well-wrapped corpse is secured with linen cords and placed within a linen shroud.

11 finishing
Adorned with a painted face mask, the body is lowered into its coffin. The jackal-headed priest places a papyrus Book of the Dead beside the body.

Saqqara's Step Pyramid

After Karnak, Dedia and his family sail to the city of Memphis to pick up a very important passenger: the regional governor. The governor is going to Piramesse to meet with the pharaoh. He isn't ready when they arrive, so the group goes on a sightseeing trip to nearby Saqqara to visit the pyramid tombs of the ancient kings of Egypt. Prince Khaemwaset has begun massive repair work there, so things are very disorganized. However, Dedia is quite proud to discover ancient graffiti.

Step Pyramid
The first pyramid was built fo King Djoser. Starting as a sto mastaba, six massive "steps" were added to create a pyramid nearly 200 feet high.

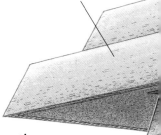

pyramid restoration
By the time of Ramses II, the Saqqara pyramid complex was over 1,000 years old. The king's fourth son, Khaemwaset, made a name for himself by restoring this and other monuments. It was a way of showing respect for his royal predecessors.

pyramid of King Unas

passage to burial chamber

burial chamber
The mummified body, its coffin, and its sarcophagus are laid deep in the burial chamber to keep them safe from robbers. The interior of King Unas's pyramid also contains the earliest-known pyramid texts—spells to help the deceased in various ways. Some of the texts were echoed in the later Book of the Dead.

mortuary temple
Deceased kings were gods. While alive, they built mortuary temples in which they could be worshipped after their death, and in which offerings could be made to sustain them in the next life.

pyramid construction
People have long wondered how pyramids were raised to such a height. The answer is probably that a massive ramp of earth, built alongside the pyramid site, was used to drag the building blocks into place.

injured worker
A construction-site doctor treats a worker with a broken arm. Egyptian doctors were skilled at dealing with fractures and similar injuries.

dead laborer

foreman

boat

boat pit of King Unas
Gods travel in holy barges, so boats were buried near the king (who has become a god) for his use in the afterlife.

causeway of Unas

relief carving

supplies

carpenters

workmen's camp and storage area

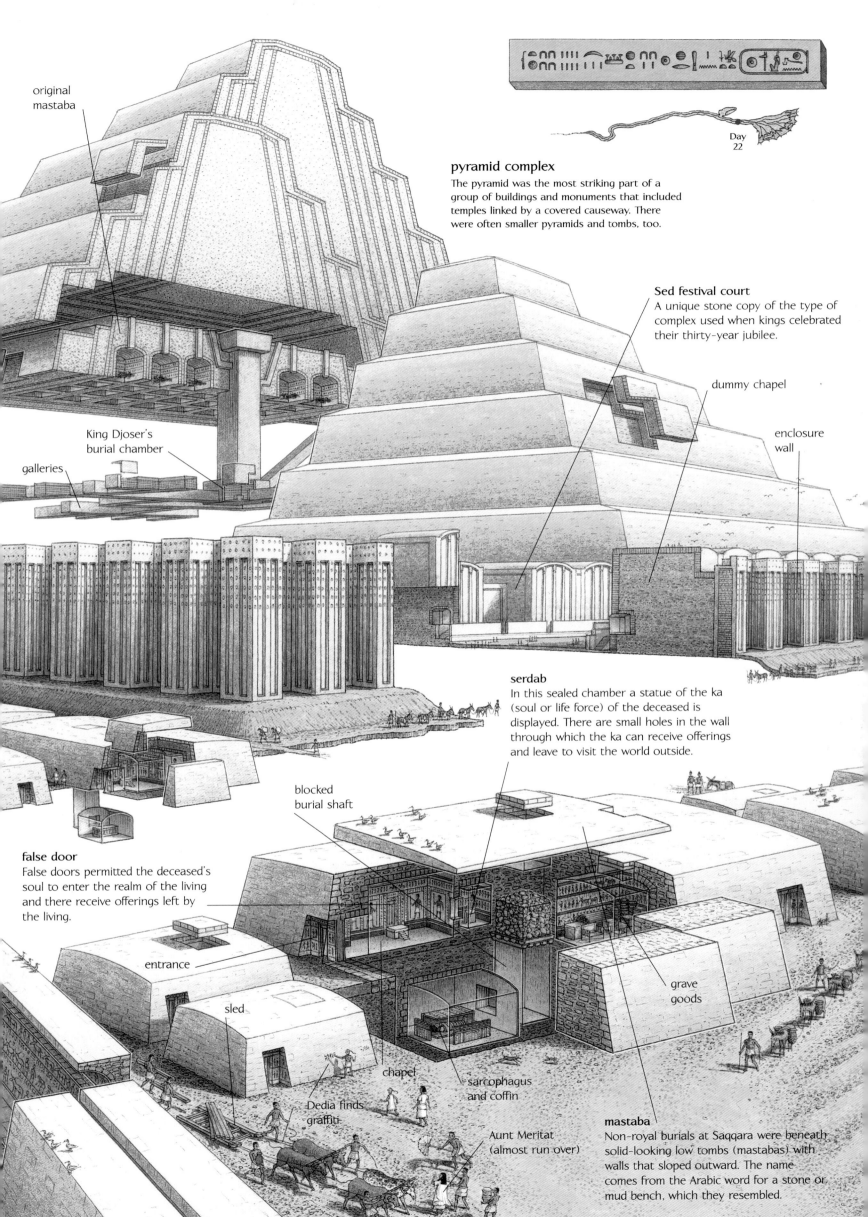

original
mastaba

pyramid complex
The pyramid was the most striking part of a
group of buildings and monuments that included
temples linked by a covered causeway. There
were often smaller pyramids and tombs, too.

Sed festival court
A unique stone copy of the type of
complex used when kings celebrated
their thirty-year jubilee.

dummy chapel

enclosure
wall

King Djoser's
burial chamber

galleries

serdab
In this sealed chamber a statue of the ka
(soul or life force) of the deceased is
displayed. There are small holes in the wall
through which the ka can receive offerings
and leave to visit the world outside.

blocked
burial shaft

false door
False doors permitted the deceased's
soul to enter the realm of the living
and there receive offerings left by
the living.

entrance

grave
goods

sled

chapel

sarcophagus
and coffin

Dedia finds
graffiti

Aunt Meritat
(almost run over)

mastaba
Non-royal burials at Saqqara were beneath
solid-looking low tombs (mastabas) with
walls that sloped outward. The name
comes from the Arabic word for a stone or
mud bench, which they resembled.

23

The fertile Nile

As Wennufer's boat sails on, Dedia watches the farmers restore their fields after the yearly floods and prepare them for sowing. One morning, as the boat passes the pyramids and Sphinx of Giza, the governor speaks to Dedia. The governor wonders whether Dedia and Ipuia would like to offer the young lion cub to the pharaoh (who is quite fond of animals). Without thinking, Dedia says he'd be delighted. When Dedia points out that the lion cub is Ipuia's, the governor smiles and says he'll settle things.

The Sphinx of Giza
"Sphinx" may have meant "living image," and the largest and best-known example probably shows the face of King Khafra. At 240 feet long and 66 feet high, it was originally carved from a single rocky outcrop. Workers are seen here replacing the Sphinx's beard.

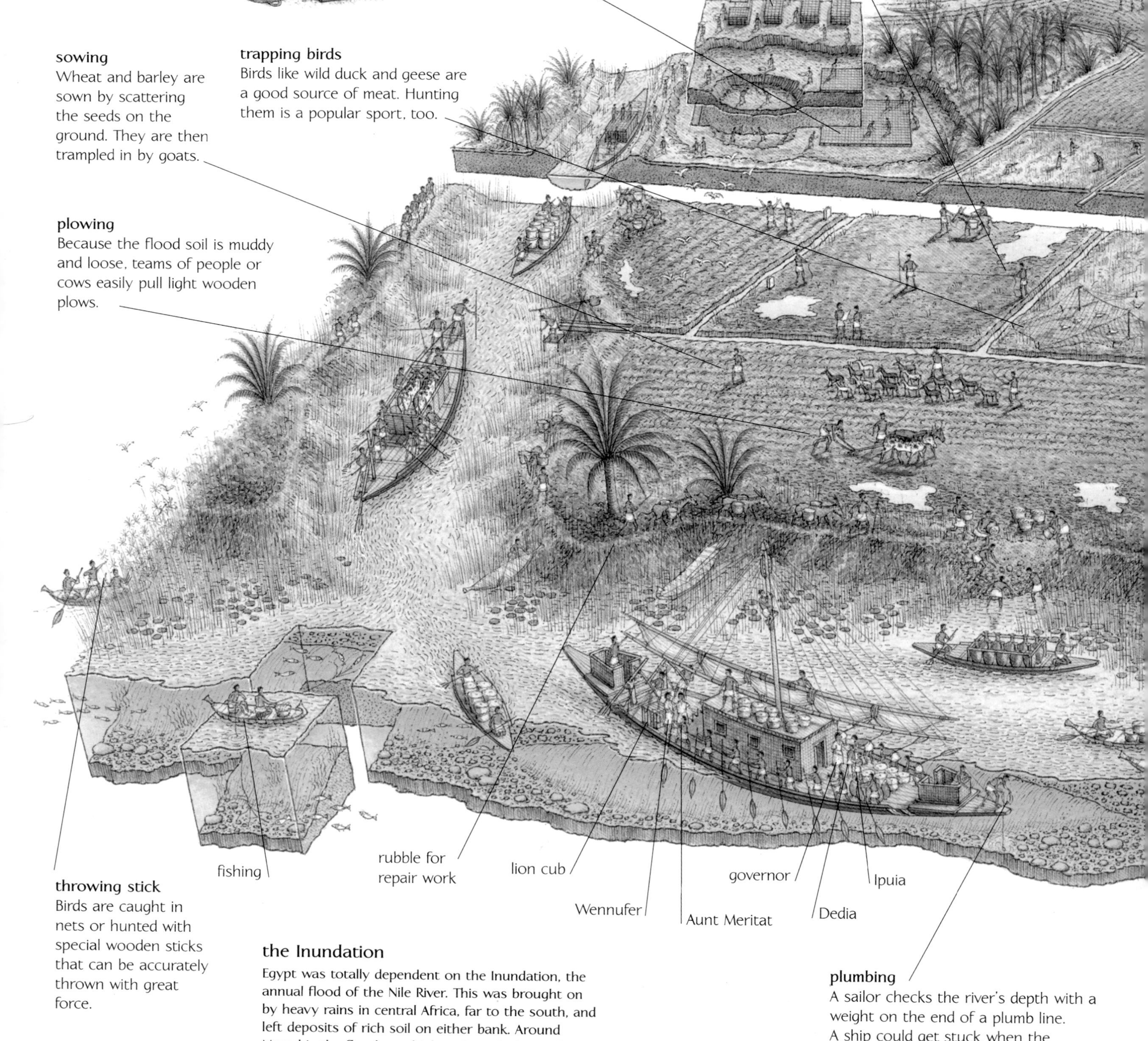

marking out the fields
As the Inundation has washed away all the old field boundaries, they are measured out again by officials known as "rope stretchers."

villa

brick-making
Bricks are made with Nile mud reinforced with straw or chaff left over from threshing grain. They are left to dry out in the hot Sun.

dried bricks

sowing
Wheat and barley are sown by scattering the seeds on the ground. They are then trampled in by goats.

trapping birds
Birds like wild duck and geese are a good source of meat. Hunting them is a popular sport, too.

plowing
Because the flood soil is muddy and loose, teams of people or cows easily pull light wooden plows.

throwing stick
Birds are caught in nets or hunted with special wooden sticks that can be accurately thrown with great force.

fishing

rubble for repair work

lion cub

Wennufer

Aunt Meritat

governor

Dedia

Ipuia

the Inundation
Egypt was totally dependent on the Inundation, the annual flood of the Nile River. This was brought on by heavy rains in central Africa, far to the south, and left deposits of rich soil on either bank. Around Memphis the flood was highest in early September.

plumbing
A sailor checks the river's depth with a weight on the end of a plumb line. A ship could get stuck when the floodwater receded.

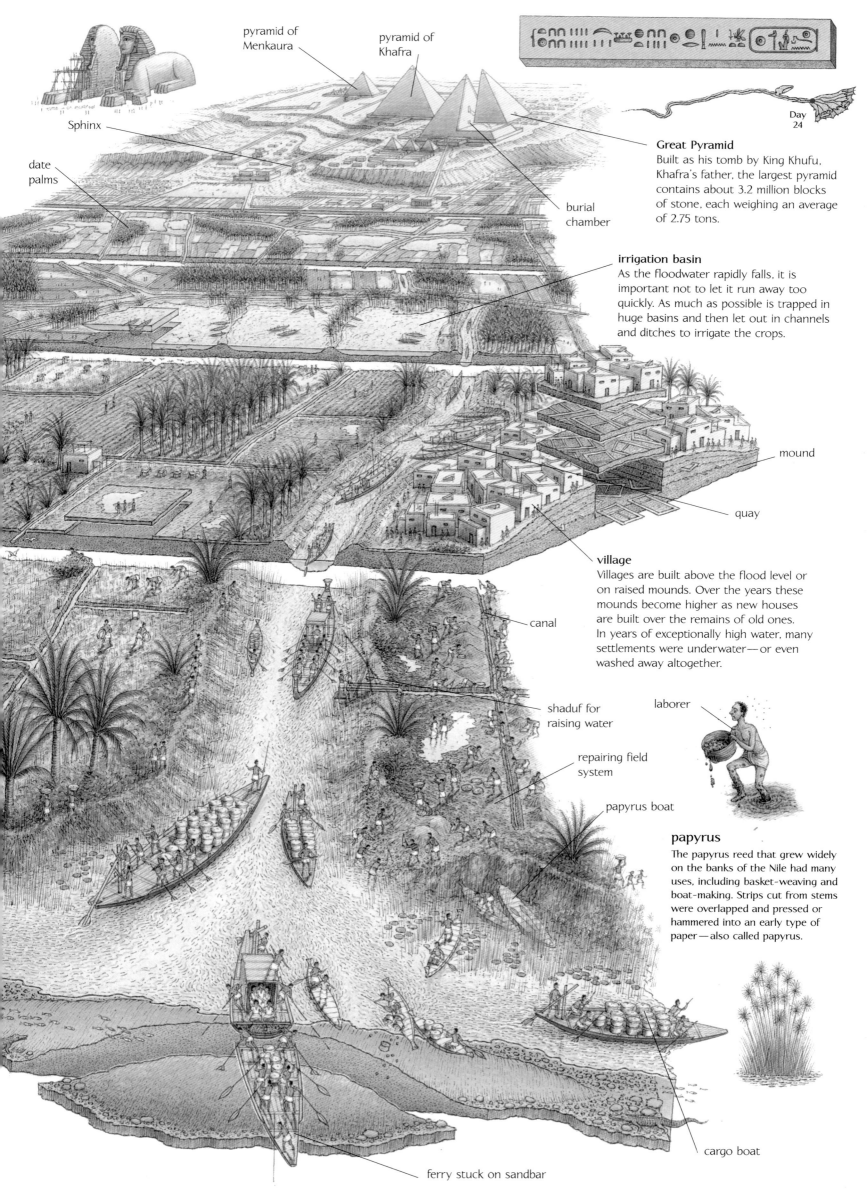

pyramid of Menkaura

pyramid of Khafra

Sphinx

date palms

burial chamber

Great Pyramid
Built as his tomb by King Khufu, Khafra's father, the largest pyramid contains about 3.2 million blocks of stone, each weighing an average of 2.75 tons.

irrigation basin
As the floodwater rapidly falls, it is important not to let it run away too quickly. As much as possible is trapped in huge basins and then let out in channels and ditches to irrigate the crops.

mound

quay

village
Villages are built above the flood level or on raised mounds. Over the years these mounds become higher as new houses are built over the remains of old ones. In years of exceptionally high water, many settlements were underwater—or even washed away altogether.

canal

shaduf for raising water

repairing field system

papyrus boat

laborer

papyrus
The papyrus reed that grew widely on the banks of the Nile had many uses, including basket-weaving and boat-making. Strips cut from stems were overlapped and pressed or hammered into an early type of paper—also called papyrus.

cargo boat

ferry stuck on sandbar

25

Ramses' palace at Piramesse

At Piramesse the regional governor has arranged for Dedia and Ipuia to present the lion cub to His Majesty *in person!* Dedia and Ipuia have an unforgettable experience as they walk through the palace courtyards and into the pharaoh's throne room. What's more, His Majesty presents Ipuia with a beautiful necklace. Afterward, having shared so many adventures together, Ipuia and Dedia become quite good friends.

Ramses the Great

Ramses II is known as "the Great" because, during his extraordinary sixty-seven-year reign, he constructed a range of buildings all over Egypt and reestablished Egyptian peace and prosperity.

Ramses II

throne room

The throne room is like the inner sanctuary of a temple, with the king-god himself seated on a raised platform at the far end.

pharaoh

The importance of the king's palace (*per-aa* or "great house") is shown by the fact that the name eventually became the title of the king himself—pharaoh.

wife

Bint-Anath, the king's favorite wife, sits on his left.

fan-bearer

floor tiles

The floor tiles are decorated with images of the king's enemies so that everyone entering walks all over them!

instruments

The Egyptians loved music and played a variety of instruments, including drums, tambourines, flutes, and lutes.

pillared hall

The entire palace, but especially the pillared hall, is decorated with scenes that remind the viewer that the king is the source of fertility, wealth, and plenty.

mud-plaster coating

rush matting

dancers

acrobats

governor and lion cub

Wennufer

Dedia and Ipuia

Day 30

tribute

Foreigners deliver tribute. Like other powerful kings, Ramses demands regular payment from the subjects within his widespread empire.

courtiers

The royal court was like a small village. It was populated by the royal family, high priests, nobles, scribes, officials, entertainers, guards, and servants.

palace pool

Complete with ducks, fish, and water lilies, the pool is a reminder of the sacredness of water in a barren land.

mandrake

ivory

date palm

inlaid pavement

palm-style columns around courtyard

palace guard

Ramses can call on an enormous army of perhaps 20,000 soldiers. Only the elite, however, are selected to be one of his personal bodyguards.

standard-bearer

bugler

drummer

entertainment

Because their religion paid so much attention to death and rebirth, Egyptian civilization might be thought rather gloomy. Far from it! The royal court was alive with every type of delight, from dancing to board games and juggling to book collecting.

gold

pomegranate tree

ostrich

royal menagerie

Ramses was famous for his collection of wild animals (menagerie)—which really did include a lion cub!

baboons

Glossary

afterlife: the Egyptians believed that death was just a transition between life on earth and the afterlife. Descriptions of the latter vary: from people becoming stars to their continuing to live an earth-style life in the fertile Field of Reeds.

Amduat: a text describing the nightly journey of the Sun through the Duat, the dark underworld region beneath the earth.

amulet: a small charm with magic or holy power, often in the shape of a sacred animal or object. It was worn to protect its owner or to give the wearer special strength.

Book of Gates: a text guiding a deceased person through the complex network of doors and passageways of the Underworld to the chamber where he or she would be judged.

Book of the Dead: a collection of up to 190 spells, often written on papyrus and placed inside a coffin, to assist a deceased person in his or her quest to enter the afterlife.

canopic jar: one of a set of four jars, stored within a canopic chest, in which were kept the preserved internal organs of a mummified body (except the heart and kidneys, which remained with the body).

cataract: rocky rapids that make a river impassable to boats.

hieroglyphs: ancient Egypt's complex system of writing used three types of hieroglyphic symbols. Some were diagrams of the thing they represented; others represented sounds or ideas. Modern scholars could not read hieroglyphic writing until the discovery in 1799 and deciphering in 1822 of the Rosetta stone—an artifact inscribed with the same text in three languages, including hieroglyphs and the familiar ancient Greek.

hypostyle: a court filled with many columns. These represented reeds growing around the mound from which the earth had been made at the time of creation.

Inundation: the annual flooding of the Nile's banks, as waters rushed down from the African highlands to the south. The Egyptians gave great religious significance to this seemingly miraculous event that brought life to an otherwise barren desert.

ka: a person's life force. As long as it was fed and cherished, the ka might live on after earthly death. When this happened, it also protected and nourished the deceased person's body.

mastaba: a solid-looking low tomb with outward-sloping walls. Some of the earliest royal burials were made beneath these bench-shaped structures.

natron: a compound of sodium that occurred in and around the sites of Egypt's prehistoric lakes. It was used for all kinds of cleaning purposes, most famously for drying out a corpse for mummification.

Nilometer: a device, often consisting of simple steps leading down to the water, by which the level of the Nile River was measured. It is not clear why this information was needed, but it seems to have been for religious, taxation, or agricultural purposes.

obelisk: a needle-shaped stone monument connected to Sun worship. Baboons, famous for getting excited at sunrise, were often carved around the foot of an obelisk.

papyrus: a large, dense reed that grew beside the Nile and had many uses. It was woven into baskets and boats, and hammered into an early form of paper.

pharaoh: often used rather inaccurately to refer to any Egyptian ruler, pharaoh originally meant the royal palace (*per-aa* or "great house"). By the middle of the second millennium BCE, it was being used for the monarch (male or female) who occupied that house.

pigment: natural coloring that was mixed with oil or water to make paint or ink.

pylon: a huge, highly decorated gateway representing the pillars of the horizon through which the Sun rose each day. It had two tapering towers linked by a lower bridge-type construction.

pyramidion: a single pyramid-shaped stone placed at the top of a pyramid or obelisk. Many were gilded—covered in a thin layer of gold that shone in the rays of the Sun.

sarcophagus: a container, usually of stone, in which one or more coffins were stored for protection. The sarcophagus was normally carved and sometimes painted.

scribe: a respected professional writer who had mastered the complicated system of hieroglyphic writing.

senet: a popular game in which each player had seven pieces on a board of thirty squares in three rows of ten. Moves were determined by chance, and the object seems to have been to guide one's pieces along a twisting path—a bit like a sophisticated kind of snakes and ladders.

serdab: a room in a mastaba tomb where a statue of the deceased's ka was usually placed. The chamber wall had one or more small openings for offerings to be passed in and through which the ka could venture out.

shaduf: a device for lifting water that has been in use for thousands of years. The scoop on one end of a hinged pole is counterbalanced by a weight on the other.

shrine: an Egyptian temple was believed to be the place where a deity actually lived. The shrine was the inner chamber where his or her image was tended by priests.

sphinx: a creature with the head of a human or other animal and the body of a lion. It was associated with the king and Sun worship.

stela: a stone or wood slab on which paintings, carvings, or writings were displayed. They were often associated with caring for the dead.

tribute: payment made to a conquering power. When its empire was at its furthest extent, tribute poured into Egypt from all around the Near East.

Underworld: known as the Duat, the Underworld was the dark region beneath the earth through which the Sun sailed each night in a boat.

Kings and queens mentioned in the text

Djoser (2667–2648 BCE) was the king for whom the Saqqara Step Pyramid was built.

Khufu (2589–2566 BCE) was the king who built the Great Pyramid of Giza.

Khafra (2558–2532 BCE), whose face is supposed to be on the Great Sphinx of Giza, was the son of Khufu.

Unas (2375–2345 BCE) was buried close to the Saqqara Step Pyramid.

Thutmose III (1479–1426 BCE), a successful warrior king, was buried in the Valley of the Kings.

Hatshepsut (1472–1458 BCE) was perhaps the most successful of all the women who ruled as pharaohs.

Ramses II (1279–1213 BCE) ruled for many years and built or took over a vast number of monuments, earning himself the title Ramses the Great.

Bint-Anath (died around 1213 BCE) was Ramses II's eldest daughter, who later became his favorite queen.

Deities mentioned in the text

Amun-Ra: Amun, whose name may mean "the hidden one," was a popular god of the Thebes region who became known as the King of the Gods. Sometimes shown with a ram's head, he was commonly linked to another popular and powerful deity, the Sun god Ra.

Anubis: the jackal-headed Anubis was god of the dead and guardian of cemeteries. Anubis was connected with mummification, and his black color was a reminder of the fertile soil found on the banks of the Nile.

Atum: an ancient creator god, Atum was also worshipped as a Sun god. Like Amun, he became closely linked with Ra, another Sun god.

Geb: a green-colored god of the earth. Geb, like Osiris, was responsible for vegetation.

Horus: the ancient falcon god Horus was a sky god and one of the protectors of Egypt's reigning king. Indeed, he was kingship itself in living form.

Khnum: the ram-headed god of Elephantine was linked to the Inundation, creativity, and pottery.

Montu: another falcon-headed deity, Montu was the god of war.

Mut: Mut was the partner of Amun and holy mother of the ruling king. One of the daughters of the Sun, she was shown brightly clothed with a vulture headdress.

Nut: Nut was the sky goddess, whose body arched like the sky overhead. Some traditions said she swallowed the setting Sun every evening and gave birth to it again each morning. She was the sisterwife of the Earth god Geb.

Osiris: One of the earliest and most important Egyptian gods, Osiris was commonly shown as a royal mummy. He was associated with death, rebirth, and fertility and was commonly colored green (vegetation) or black (soil). He fathered the falcon god Horus.

Index

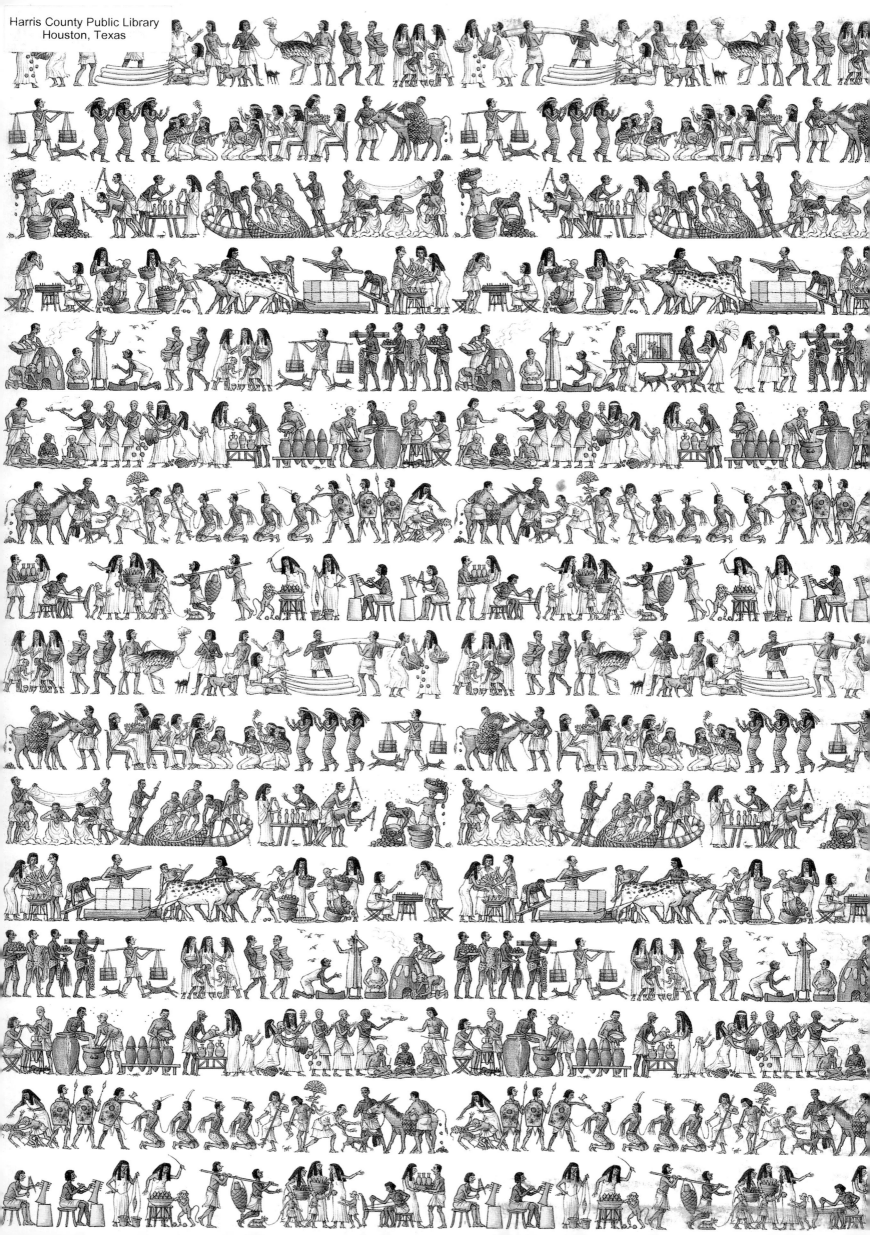